MACMILLAN READERS

ELEMENTARY LEVEL

KU-365-216

MEG CABOT

The
Princess Diaries 2

Retold by Anne Collins

MACMILLAN

70001617685 9

Contents

Notes About The Author and This Story

Meg Cabot (Meggin Patricia Cabot) was born in Bloomington, Indiana, U.S.A. She lives in New York City with her husband, Benjamin, and her cat, Henrietta. She studied Art at Indiana University. Then she became an illustrator of books and magazines.

Meg's first novel, *Where Roses Grow Wild*, was published in 1988. She wrote this book using the name Patricia Cabot. Her favorite authors are Jane Austen, Judy Blume, and Barbara Cartland. Her favorite food is pizza.

Some of Meg Cabot's stories are: *The Princess Diaries* (2000), *The Princess Diaries:Take Two* (2000), *The Princess Diaries:Third Time Lucky* (2001), *The Princess Diaries:Mia Goes Forth* (2002), *The Princess Diaries:Give Me Five* (2003). The first two stories about Princess Mia were made into the movie, *The Princess Diaries* (Buena Vista/Walt Disney Pictures, 2001).

ecology the study of life on Earth and the way that people, animals and plants live together.

e-mail a way of sending messages from one computer to another. E-mail messages can be sent on the Internet to **chatrooms**. You can have a conversation in an Internet chatroom because the computer messages are instant.

Halloween the night of October 31st. People used to believe that the spirits of the dead walked about on this night. At Halloween parties, people wear costumes of demons, ghosts, vampires, and other frightening creatures.

online use a computer to talk to people on a computer network, and to search for information on the Internet.

Picture Dictionary

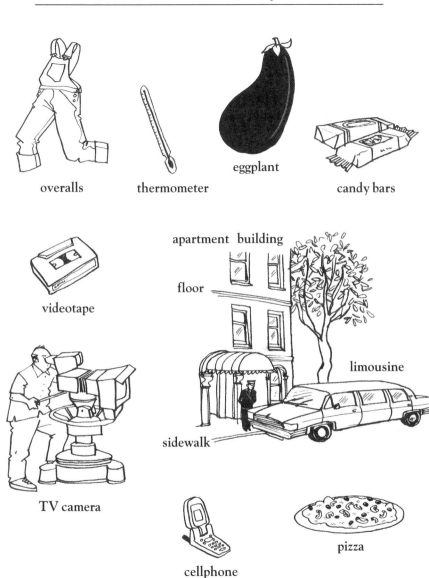

overalls

thermometer

eggplant

candy bars

videotape

apartment building

floor

limousine

TV camera

sidewalk

cellphone

pizza

The People in This Story

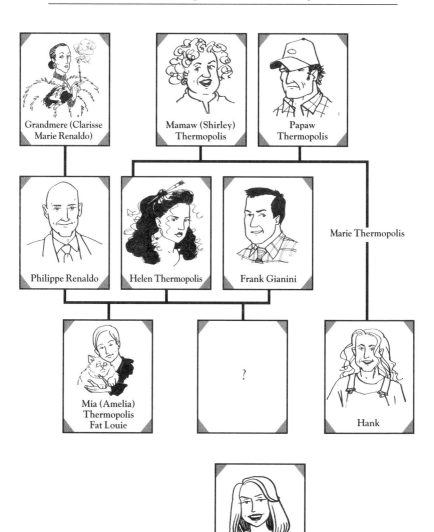

Grandmere (Clarisse Marie Renaldo)

Mamaw (Shirley) Thermopolis

Papaw Thermopolis

Philippe Renaldo

Helen Thermopolis

Frank Gianini

Marie Thermopolis

Mia (Amelia) Thermopolis Fat Louie

?

Hank

Beverley Bellerieve

Doctor Moscovitz

Doctor Moscovitz

Josh Richter

Lana Weinberger

Michael Moscovitz

Lilly Moscovitz

Boris Pelkowski

Kenny Showalter

Tina Hakim Baba

Shameeka Taylor

Ling Su

Principal Gupta

Wahim

Lars

Vigo

1

The Private Diary of an "Ordinary" Teenager

My name is Mia Thermopolis and this is my diary. Some things about my life are very ordinary. I'm fourteen years old, and I live in New York City. I live in an apartment in Greenwich Village, on the west side of the city. I live with my mom, Helen, and my cat, Fat Louie. My mom is an artist. She paints pictures.

I'm a freshman—a ninth grade student at Albert Einstein High School. My friends, Tina Hakim Baba, Shameeka Taylor, Ling Su, and Lilly Moscovitz are also in the ninth grade. Lilly is my best friend.

Other things about my life aren't ordinary at all. Last month, I heard some amazing news. I'm not just an ordinary teenager, I'm also a princess! I'm the

Princess of Genovia. Genovia is a small country in Europe near the border of France and Italy. My dad, Philippe Renaldo, is the Prince of Genovia and I'm his heir. When he dies, I'll become the ruler of Genovia. Every day after school finishes, I have princess classes with my dad's mother, Grandmere.

Grandmere is the Dowager Princess of Genovia. She is teaching me to be a princess. Grandmere wears purple clothes and she smokes cigarettes all the time. She speaks French and wears lots of makeup. She is scary—everyone is frightened of her.

My mom and dad never got married, but they're still friends. Mom is dating my Algebra teacher, Mr Frank Gianini—she's going out with him. I'm happy for her. I like Mr Gianini, but I don't like Algebra. I'm flunking Algebra—I fail every Algebra test. So I have extra Algebra classes.

Sometimes Lilly's brother, Michael, helps me with my Algebra. I've got a crush on Michael. I love him, but he doesn't know about my feelings. I'd like to go out on a date with Michael.

Monday, October 20th. 8:00 a.m.

I'VE JUST HAD A BIG SHOCK! I was eating breakfast, when my mom came into the kitchen. She had just come out of the bathroom. Her face was very pale and her hair looked terrible.

"Are you sick, Mom?" I asked her. "Do you have a headache? Do you want some aspirin?"

"No. No thanks," said my mom. Her voice was really weird. It sounded strange. I was very worried.

"What's the problem, Mom?" I asked. "What's wrong?"

"Mia, I'm pregnant!" said my mom in a shocked voice.

Suddenly her eyes were full of tears, but she was smiling. "I'm going to have a baby!"

I can't believe it. My mom is having a BABY! And its father is Mr Gianini, my Algebra teacher!

My mom and dad weren't married when I was born. Fourteen and a half years ago, Mom and Dad fell out of love with each other. My mom didn't want to marry my dad. So she became a single parent. She looked after me without anyone's help. I live with Mom in America, and my dad lives in Genovia. My dad sends us money each month.

Why wasn't Mom more careful? She is an adult, but sometimes she behaves like a teenager. She doesn't think carefully. And now she's going to be a single parent *again*.

<u>My problems</u>

1. I'm the tallest girl in the freshman class.
2. I'm a freak—I look strange. I'm very thin and I have huge feet.
3. Last month, my mom started dating my Algebra teacher.
4. Last month, my dad told me, "You are the Princess of Genovia."
5. I have princess classes with my scary grandmother.
6. In December, I must go on TV in Genovia. I have to introduce myself to the Genovian people.
7. I don't have a boyfriend.

Algebra class

Mr Gianini hasn't spoken to me about Mom's pregnancy. Maybe my mom hasn't told him about the baby.

What will my new baby brother or baby sister look like? My mom is very beautiful. She has thick, black, curly hair. Mr Gianini is tall and good-looking, and he's very smart. Maybe the baby will be smart too. But I want the baby to have my mom's nose. Mr Gianini's nose is too long.

English class

Mrs Spears, our English teacher, has given us a new project. We have to write a diary. She wants to read our diaries and know more about us. But I write *this* diary every day. My mom gave me this diary about a month ago. She was worried about me. I never talked about my feelings. She wanted me to write down my feelings.

I don't want Mrs Spears to read this diary. My thoughts are private. I don't want Mrs Spears to read my secrets. I'll have to start a different diary for Mrs Spears. It'll be a fake diary. I won't write about my real feelings in the fake diary.

Mrs Spears wants us to write about ourselves at the beginning of our diaries. This is what I'll write for my introduction:

ENGLISH PROJECT: MY DIARY
by Mia Thermopolis

Name: My full name is Princess Amelia Mignonette Grimaldi Thermopolis Renaldo of Genovia. When people speak to me they call me, "Your Highness." In America, I'm sometimes called "Princess Mia." A month ago, everyone called me Mia (or Amelia) Thermopolis. My friends call me "Mia."

Age: 14

School Grade: Freshman—ninth grade.

Description: I'm five feet and nine inches tall. My eyes are gray and my feet are too large. My hair is short and very curly. The real color of my hair is light brown. But last month, I went to a beauty salon. Paolo, the stylist, cut my hair and colored it blond. I'm a vegetarian—I don't eat meat.

Parents: My mother's name is Helen Thermopolis. She's an artist. My father's full name is Artur Christoff Philippe Gerard Grimaldi Renaldo. He is the Prince of Genovia.

Pets: Fat Louie—an orange and white cat. Fat Louie is eight years old and he weighs 25 pounds.

Best Friend: Lilly Moscovitz. Lilly is very smart and she's interested in politics and ecology. She cares about people and what happens to the planet Earth. She makes films about the people of New York, and their problems. She has her own TV show—*Lilly Tells It Like It Is*.

Boyfriend: I don't have one.

Address: 1005 Thompson Street, Apartment 4A, New York. I've lived all my life in New York City with my mother. But every summer I go to France and visit my father. We stay in my grandmother's house.

About a month ago, my father told me, "Mia, I am the Prince of Genovia. You are my heir." After that, he came to stay at the Plaza Hotel in New York. He's staying in a suite in the penthouse—rooms on the hotel's top floor. My grandmother has a suite in the penthouse too. I have to go there every afternoon. My grandmother is teaching me how to be a princess.

———

Afternoon

Lilly sat with me in the cafeteria during lunch.

"What's wrong, Mia?" she asked. "Something's wrong."

I wanted to say, "Lilly, my mom's PREGNANT!" But I didn't say this. I told a lie. "Nothing's wrong," I said. But Lilly didn't believe me.

I'm worried about my mom and Mr Gianini. Will Grandmere be mad about my mom's pregnancy? Will she be angry when she hears the news about the baby? And what about my dad? How will he feel? Will he be angry? Or will he be sad? A year ago, my dad got very sick. He had cancer. Dad is OK now, but he can't have any more children. He's not in love with my mom now, but maybe this news will hurt him.

And has Mom thought about which foods are best for a pregnant woman? My mom doesn't eat healthy foods. She eats too many candy bars, cakes and pizzas, and she drinks beer. Our refrigerator is full of the wrong kinds of food. I must throw out all the alcohol and coffee. I must buy fresh fruit, vegetables and milk.

Late afternoon

Today, I used the school computer and I went on the Internet. I found some information about pregnancy. Lilly saw what I was looking at.

"Do you have a secret to tell me, Mia?" she said in a shocked voice. "Are you *pregnant?*"

Lilly's voice is very loud. Everyone heard her.

"I'm looking for some information for my Biology class," I said. Only part of this was true. I'm working on a special project with Kenny Showalter. Kenny is my study partner in Biology class. The project isn't about pregnant women. It's about insects. But Lilly doesn't know this.

Lilly went on talking about pregnancy. I was very embarrassed because her brother, Michael, was sitting with us. He heard our conversation. I wanted Lilly to shut up.

I've liked Michael for a long time. But he doesn't know this. He's a senior student—he's older than me. He's very smart and he's kind. He's also good-looking, and he has a gorgeous body. But Michael doesn't notice me at all. I'm just his younger sister's best friend.

2

Grandmere's Surprise

Monday, October 20th. After school

When I got home, there was a phone message on the answering machine. Grandmere had called while we were out.

"My plans have changed," she said in her message. "I was going away for a few days. But now I have decided to stay in New York. Call me back immediately, Amelia. I have a surprise for you."

What is Grandmere's surprise? It's something horrible, I'm sure. I'm not going to call her back. If she calls again, I'll tell a lie. I'll say, "I didn't get your message. The answering machine didn't work properly."

Early evening

Grandmere called again.

"Come and have dinner with me and your father tonight at the Plaza Hotel," she said. "I'll tell you about your surprise then."

My mom has invited Mr Gianini to our apartment this evening. She is going to tell him about the baby. I *will* go to the Plaza and have dinner with Dad and Grandmere.

Late evening—11:00 p.m.

I now know all about Grandmere's surprise, and I don't like

it. I'm going to be on a TV show called *Twenty-Four/Seven*. Lots of people in America watch this show every week. *Twenty-Four/Seven* is very popular.

Grandmere spoke to the people who work on the show. She made an arrangement with them. I'm going to be interviewed by Beverly Bellerieve. Beverly is going to ask me questions about being a princess. The interview will be filmed next Saturday.

I don't want to be on the *Twenty-Four/Seven* show. But Grandmere won't listen to me. "You have to tell everybody about Genovia," she said. "Then lots of tourists will go there. This will be very good for Genovia."

"Your grandmother is right, Mia," said my dad. Then he started asking questions about the interviewer, Beverly Bellerieve.

"Didn't she win the Miss America beauty competition in 1991?" he said. "Is she dating anyone?" My dad likes beautiful women.

"Where will the interview be filmed?" I asked. "Will it be filmed at my apartment, or at the Plaza Hotel?"

Then I thought about my mom and Mr Gianini.

"What will Mr Gianini say when Mom tells him about the baby?" I said to myself. "Will he be happy?"

When I got back to the apartment, the door to my mom's bedroom was closed. I heard Mom and Mr Gianini talking quietly inside the room. I want Mr Gianini to be pleased about the baby. He's the best guy that my mother has ever dated.

I went into my bedroom and switched on my computer. There was an e-mail message from Michael Moscovitz. He wanted to talk to me. Michael likes working on computers. He is a member of the Computer Club at school. He writes an online magazine called *Crackhead*.

Michael and I often use our computers to send instant messages to each other. We have conversations in an Internet chatroom. We use different names when we chat to each other. I use the name "FtLouie." It means Fat Louie. It's the name of my cat. Michael uses the name "CracKing"—a criminal who sells drugs. Michael is always making clever jokes. This was our conversation:

```
CracKing: At school today you were weird. What's wrong
with you?
FtLouie: Nothing is wrong. I'm fine.
CracKing: You weren't listening when I was helping you
with your Algebra problems.
FtLouie: Yes, I was. I heard everything that you said.
```

But I wasn't telling Michael the truth. There is something wrong. I have a problem, and I can't talk to him about it. I HAVE A CRUSH ON MICHAEL MOSCOVITZ! When I'm close to Michael, I can't think clearly. He makes me feel happy and excited.

I have to stop writing now. My mom is outside my room. She's knocking at the door.

Very late

My mom just came into my bedroom and she was crying.

"Why are you crying?" I asked. "Isn't Mr Gianini pleased about the baby? What did he say?"

"I'm crying because I'm so happy," she replied.

Then she pulled me into the living room. Mr Gianini was standing there.

"We want you to hear our news first," said my mom. "We're getting married."

Then she put her arms around me and held me tightly. Mr Gianini hugged me too. It's very weird, being hugged by your Algebra teacher!

Tuesday, October 21st, 1:00 a.m.

MY MOM AND MR GIANINI ARE GETTING MARRIED! Does my mom believe in marriage? She never married my dad. Maybe he never asked her.

I've just realized something. If my mom marries Mr Gianini, he'll live with us. He'll live here, in this apartment. I'll have to eat breakfast every morning WITH MY ALGEBRA TEACHER!

9:00 a.m.

When I woke up this morning, my throat was painful. I felt ill and I couldn't talk properly. I tried to shout for my mom, but my voice was very weak. She couldn't hear me. So I got up and went down the hall to her room.

"Mom, I'm sick," I whispered. "I can't go to school today. Please will you call the school? And please call Lars. Tell him, 'Don't come with the limousine.' And call Lilly."

Lars is my driver and bodyguard. His job is to protect me because I'm a princess. He drives me to school every day in my dad's limousine. We always pick up Lilly and take her to school too.

Late morning

My mom usually goes to her art studio to paint. But today she stayed at home and looked after me. She made me cups of tea and special food.

At ten o'clock, Mom put a thermometer in my mouth. She took my temperature. She wanted to find out if my body heat was normal. After a minute, she took the thermometer out of my mouth and looked at it.

"Your temperature is ninety-nine point zero degrees," she said. "It is zero point six degrees higher than normal." Then she touched my face. "Your skin is hot. You have a fever. Stay in bed and rest."

My temperature:
11:45 a.m.—99.2°F
12:14 p.m.—99.1°F
1:27 p.m.—98.6°F
2:05 p.m.—99.0°F
3:35 p.m.—99.1°F

Maybe my temperature won't be normal by Saturday. Then I can't be interviewed by Beverly Bellerieve. GREAT!

Evening
Grandmere called a short time ago. "I'm sick," I told her. But she didn't feel sorry for me at all.

"If I'm still sick on Saturday, I won't be able to do the interview," I said.

"Of course you will," said Grandmere. "A princess must do her duties for her people, even if she is sick."

Wednesday, October 22nd
When I woke up, my temperature was 102°F! My mom called my dad. She asked him to take me to my doctor. So Lars and my dad came to the apartment in the limousine.

We had to sit in the doctor's reception for about ten minutes before the doctor examined me. My dad spent the ten minutes talking to the doctor's pretty receptionist.

The doctor looked inside my throat and felt my neck.

"You have a throat infection," he said.

Then he wrote a prescription for some medicine. "Take this," he said, giving me the piece of paper. "Go to a drug store and buy this medicine. You must take the medicine four times each day. When your temperature is normal, you can go to school."

18

As soon as I got home, I took some of the medicine. Then I went to bed.

My temperature:

5:20 p.m.—99.3°F

6:45 p.m.—99.2°F

7:52 p.m.—99.1°F

My temperature is starting to go down. I don't want to get better too quickly! If I'm better by Saturday, I'll have to do that stupid interview.

3

A Secret Admirer

Thursday, October 23rd

This morning, something very exciting happened.

My mom brought me a letter that came in the mail. When I opened the envelope, I got a big surprise. Someone has sent me a LOVE LETTER! I don't know who sent it, there was no name at the end. It was from a secret admirer. The person wanted to keep his name a secret. The letter was signed, "A Friend." It was printed on a computer. There was no handwriting on it. This is what it said:

Dear Mia,

I feel strange writing this letter. But I'm too shy to talk to you. I can't tell you my real feelings. So I'm writing my feelings in this letter. I've liked you for a very long time. I liked you before you became a princess. I'll always like you.

Sincerely,

A Friend

I've never had a letter like this before! Is it from Michael Moscovitz? I hope that it is. But Michael sees me nearly every day. And he's never spoken to me about his feelings. If the letter isn't from Michael, who sent it?

I want to call Lilly, Tina and Shameeka and tell them about the letter. But they are in school. I CAN'T BE SICK NOW! I have to get well immediately. I want to go back to school and find out about this letter.

My temperature:

10:45 p.m.—99.2°F
11:15 p.m.—99.1°F
12:27 p.m.—98.6°F

Yes! YES! I'm getting better!

2:05 p.m.—99.0°F.

Oh no! My temperature is going up again!

3:35 p.m.—99.1°F.

I'm not getting better! Why is this happening to me?

Late afternoon

Lilly came to the apartment after school. She bought some homework for me.

I didn't tell Lilly about the letter. I won't tell anyone. A love letter is very private. Maybe Michael did write it. If he wrote it, he won't want everyone to know about it.

Lilly sat on my bed and we watched a movie on TV. The movie was about a handsome boy who fell in love with a girl. Later, the boy found out that the girl was a princess. Her story was just like mine! But the girl in the movie couldn't marry the handsome boy. Her father had arranged for her to marry a prince.

"Maybe my dad has arranged a royal marriage for me too," I said to Lilly. "So I can't fall in love with a handsome actor, or your brother Michael. I'll have to marry someone like Prince William, and live in Britain."

Lilly looked at me, then she went into the living room.

My father was sitting there, reading a newspaper. He was looking after me for a few hours. My mom wasn't in the apartment. She didn't want to tell Dad about her marriage to Mr Gianini, or her pregnancy. She had gone shopping.

"Mr Renaldo," I heard Lilly say. "Is Mia secretly engaged to be married? Is she going to be married to a prince, or a millionaire?"

"No, of course not," said my dad.

Lilly came back into my bedroom. "You're worried about falling in love with an actor. I understand that," she said. "But why did you talk about love and my brother Michael?"

Immediately, I realized my mistake. I don't want Lilly to know my feelings about her brother. I didn't answer her question.

Evening

After dinner, I switched on my computer and read my e-mail. Lots of my friends had sent me messages. There was a message from Tina Hakim Baba. "Get well soon," she said. Another friend, Shameeka, sent me an invitation to her party. Michael had sent a message too. It was a little film with a cat in it—a cat like Fat Louie. The cat was dancing and it was really cute. Michael had signed the message: *Love, Michael.*

Did Michael send me the love letter on Thursday? Is he the shy friend? I don't know. The word *love* wasn't in that letter. The sender of the letter—"A Friend"—used the word *liked*. And he signed it, "Sincerely."

Then I saw another e-mail. I didn't recognize the e-mail address. It was from someone using the name, JoCrox. Who is Jo Crox? Is he the person who sent the love letter? Is he my secret admirer? Is he the boy who likes me? This was the message:

JoCrox: I hoped to see you in class today. Then I heard about your throat infection. Are you feeling better? Did you get my letter? Get well soon.
Your Friend

Jo Crox is my secret admirer! But who *is* he? He wanted to see me in class. So we must take a class together. But there is no one in any of my classes with the name Jo.

Maybe Jo Crox isn't his real name. I looked at the name and thought for a few minutes. Then I understood! JoCrox. Jo-C-rox. Jo-see-rocks. Josie Rocks! Josie is the name of my favorite character, Josie, in the TV show *Josie and the Pussycats*. Josie "rocks" means Josie is cool. This person is saying, "Josie is cool." This person must know me well! I replied immediately.

FtLouie: Dear Friend,
I got your letter. Thank you very much. Who are you? I won't tell anyone. Please tell me. I'll keep your secret.

I waited for about half an hour, but Jo-C-rox didn't write back.

Friday, October 24th. Algebra class

I AM BETTER! My temperature is normal now, so I went to school. Lars drove me in the limousine and we picked up Lilly outside her apartment. Michael was with her. When we got to school, Michael walked with me to my class. I felt very happy.

Lilly's boyfriend, Boris Pelkowski, meets her outside school every morning and walks with her to class.

Afternoon

<u>My list of things to do</u>

1. Stop thinking so much about Jo-C-rox.
2. Stop thinking so much about Michael Moscovitz.
3. Stop thinking about my mom and her pregnancy.
4. Stop thinking about my TV interview tomorrow.
5. Stop thinking about Grandmere.
6. Stop biting my fingernails.
7. Work harder in my Algebra class.

Evening

Homework: English project. I have to write in my school diary. I have to write 200 words, with the title: *Describe a special experience that changed your life.* What can I write about? A month ago, my father told me who I was. I'm a princess. I'm heir to the throne of Genovia. My life changed then. Maybe I'll write about that.

Kenny Showalter, my partner in Biology class, had a very special experience last year. Last summer, Kenny visited India with his family. While he was there, he got very sick. He nearly died.

"That experience changed me," said Kenny. "Now, I want to help people who are sick and dying."

I've never had any experiences like that. My experiences aren't special at all.

—

4

Me and My Big Mouth

Saturday, October 25th. Grandmere's suite, the Plaza Hotel
As I waited to start my interview with Beverly Bellerieve, I felt weak and ill. My throat hurt and my body was hot.

Maybe I didn't feel well because I was nervous. *Twenty-four/Seven* is a VERY popular TV show. My interview is going to be shown on Monday night. People in about twenty-two million homes all over America will watch it.

When I got to the Plaza Hotel, my dad was in my grandmother's suite. He started talking about Mr Gianini.

"Mia, is your Algebra teacher living in your apartment?" he asked.

I didn't know what to say. Mr Gianini isn't living in our apartment. Not really. But he will be living there soon.

"Er. . .no," I said.

Dad looked happy when he heard that. But will he be happy when he finds out about Mom's marriage to Mr Gianini? Will he be happy about Mom's baby?

The interviewer, Beverly Bellerieve, arrived at the suite. She's very smart and very beautiful. My dad likes her very much. He smiled a lot when he talked to her. She smiled too. Lots of women like my dad. He's rich and he looks like Captain Jean-Luc Picard in the TV show, *Star Trek: The Next Generation*.

7:00 p.m. In the limousine
I'm feeling much worse. The interview was *awful*. I made a REALLY BAD mistake!

My dad and Grandmere watched while Beverly Bellerieve interviewed me. At first, everything went really well. But then I said a stupid thing. And because of this, my dad knows about Mom and Mr Gianini. I didn't want this to happen. I was just so nervous. Beverly was nice to me. But I couldn't think clearly and my answers were too long.

We talked for about an hour. Then Beverly said, "Mia, didn't you have some exciting news recently?"

I was very surprised. "She's asking me about the baby and the wedding," I thought.

"Oh, yes," I said quickly. "I'm very excited. I've always wanted to be a big sister. But my mom and her boyfriend don't want a big wedding. They just want a small quiet wedding."

Me and my big mouth. The words just came out! I spoke before I thought about the question.

My dad was drinking a glass of water. He dropped the glass. Grandmere started making strange noises.

Suddenly I realized what I'd said. "Oh no!" I thought. "I've said the wrong thing."

Beverly wasn't talking about my mom. She didn't know about my mom's marriage to Mr Gianini. And she didn't know about the baby. Beverly was talking about my work at school. I'd gotten a very good grade in my last Algebra test.

My dad put his hands on his head. His face was pale. He looked shocked.

What will my mom say when she finds out?

"Don't worry, Mia," said my dad. "I'll explain to your mother what happened. It wasn't your fault."

I don't know what I said in the rest of the interview. I don't remember what other questions Beverly Bellerieve asked me.

"I'm not jealous of Mr Gianini," my dad said to me later. "I'm pleased for your mother. She and Mr Gianini will be very happy." He said that, but I don't believe him.

I'm going straight from the hotel to Lilly's place. She's asked all her friends to go to her apartment. We're helping her to make a film tonight. It's about teenagers behaving badly. Maybe I can stay at Lilly's place tonight. I don't want to go home and see my mom yet. I'll wait until Dad talks to her.

Sunday, October 26th, 2:00 a.m. Lilly's bedroom

I did a very stupid thing tonight. I was with Tina, Shameeka, and Ling Su at Lilly's apartment. Lilly gave me a dare. She told me to do something stupid and dangerous.

"I want to film some teenagers behaving badly," she said. "If I ask you to do something stupid, will you do it?"

"What's the dare?" I asked.

"I dare you to drop an eggplant onto the sidewalk from my bedroom window. You won't do it. You're good. You never behave badly."

"I'll do it," I said at once. "I accept the dare."

It was a very stupid thing to do. Lilly's family live in an apartment sixteen floors up from the street. It's extremely dangerous to drop anything out of high windows in New York City. If something falls on someone in the street, they could die.

But my friends heard what Lilly said. So I agreed to do the dare. I went into Lilly's kitchen and found an eggplant. Then I went back to Lilly's bedroom. Lilly turned on her video camera and started filming.

I opened the window and dropped the eggplant. The huge purple vegetable fell down and down. Then. . .SPLAT! It hit the sidewalk. The soft eggplant exploded. Pieces of it went everywhere. Many pieces hit a bus and a Jaguar car.

I leaned out of the window. I saw a man get out of the

26

Jaguar. He looked up at Lilly's apartment building. He was trying to see which floor the eggplant came from.

Suddenly someone pulled me back. It was Michael, Lilly's brother.

"Get down!" he said. We all got down on the floor at once—me, Lilly, Michael, Shameeka, Ling Su and Tina.

I was surprised to see Michael in the apartment. I thought that he was out with his friends from the Computer Club.

"That was *really* stupid!" Michael said. "It's against the law to drop things out of windows in New York City. You could kill someone."

"Oh, don't be silly, Michael," said Lilly, laughing. "It was only a vegetable."

"I'm *not* joking, Lilly," said Michael, angrily. "I'm very serious. If anyone saw Mia do that, she'll be in big trouble. Maybe the police will arrest her. You mustn't keep that film, Lilly. No one must see the Princess of Genovia behaving so badly."

I was very pleased. Michael was trying to help me. Maybe he didn't write the love letter, but he does care about me a little.

5

Wedding Plans

Sunday, October 26th, 7:00 p.m.

I was worried. I'd told the secret about my mom and Mr Gianini. I didn't want to leave the Moscovitzes' apartment this morning. I always feel relaxed and comfortable at Lilly's place. Lilly and her family are ordinary people with normal problems. But my family is weird and our problems are always difficult.

I was surprised when I got home. My mom was happy to see me. "Don't worry, Mia," she said. "Your dad's talked to me about the TV interview. Everything's OK. I understand."

We sat down and made plans for her wedding. My mom wants to get married near the time of Halloween.

Then Lilly called.

"You've done an interview for *Twenty-Four/Seven* and it's being shown on Monday," she said. "Why didn't you tell me?"

"How do you know about this?" I asked in surprise.

"There are TV commercials advertising it," said Lilly. "They're saying, 'Princess Mia, America's royal princess, has been interviewed by Beverly Bellerieve.' Why didn't you tell me?" Lilly asked again.

"I didn't think that it was important," I said.

"You didn't think that an interview with Beverly

Bellerieve was *important*?" said Lilly. "Beverly Bellerieve is America's top TV journalist. She's great!"

"Oh," I said. "She just seemed like a nice lady."

9:00 p.m.

I've had another e-mail from Jo-C-rox!

```
JoCrox: Hi, Mia. I just saw the TV commercial for your
interview. You looked great. I'm sorry, but I can't tell
you my real name. Now stop reading your e-mail messages.
You must start your Algebra homework.
Your Friend
```

I wrote back immediately.

```
FtLouie: WHO ARE YOU?
```

Jo-C-rox didn't reply. But how does he know about my Algebra homework? Michael knows about my Algebra homework. Is he Jo-C-rox? I want Michael to be Jo-C-rox!

Monday, October 27th

Lots of people at school saw the commercials for my interview. Everyone is going to watch *Twenty-Four/Seven* tonight. Tomorrow, they'll all know about my mom and Mr Gianini. What am I going to do? What did I say in the interview? What other things did Beverly and I talk about? Did I say other stupid things?

I talked about the interview with my friend, Tina Hakim Baba. Before Tina was born, her mother was a model in Britain. She did a lot of TV interviews.

"The TV company always sent my mom a videotape of the interview before they showed the film on TV," said Tina.

This was a good idea. So at lunchtime I called my dad at the Plaza Hotel. I asked him to get a videotape of my interview from Beverly Bellerieve.

"I'll ask her now," said my dad. He spoke to someone in his hotel room. Then I heard Beverly's voice on the phone.

"What's the matter, Mia?" she asked.

Beverly was in my dad's hotel suite! I wasn't surprised. My dad liked Beverly very much when he met her.

"I'm worried about my interview," I said. "I'd like to see a videotape of the film before you show it on TV."

"You don't need to see a videotape," said Beverly. "Don't worry. Everything's fine."

Afternoon

Something very embarrassing has happened. I was walking down the school hall with Michael and Lilly, when we met Lana Weinberger. Lana is the most beautiful and popular girl in the ninth grade. Lana walked up to Michael and me and stared at us.

"Are you two dating each other?" she said loudly.

Michael's face became red. So did mine.

Lilly started to laugh. "Mia and Michael dating?" she said. "Of course they're not!"

Lana started laughing too. But Michael didn't say anything. He was putting his books in his bag.

After school

When I walked into Grandmere's hotel suite for my princess class today, she was sitting with a strange man. On the table in front of them, there was a huge piece of paper. There were lots of circles on the paper. Grandmere and the man were sticking small pieces of paper onto the circles.

"What *are* you doing, Grandmere?" I asked.

"Oh, Amelia, this is Vigo," said Grandmere, pointing to the man. "He's come here from Genovia. He plans all the important events in Genovia. He's helping me to plan your mother's wedding."

"Grandmere," I said. "Can I talk to you privately for a moment, please?"

"No," said Grandmere. "If you have anything to say, you can say it to Vigo too."

Vigo jumped up from his chair and rushed over to me. He was very short and he spoke excitedly.

"I'm delighted to meet you, Your Highness," he said.

"It's nice to meet you too," I said. "But my mom and Mr Gianini want a small, quiet wedding. I'm sure of that."

"Nonsense!" said Grandmere. "Amelia, you are a member of the Genovian royal family. One day, you'll be the

31

ruler of Genovia. Your mother must have a big wedding. The marriage will take place in the White and Gold Room here at the Plaza. Then there will be a party in the Grand Ballroom."

"Er...Grandmere," I said. "Mom and Mr Gianini don't want a big wedding and a large party."

"Why not?" said Grandmere in a surprised voice. "Your father is paying for everything, of course."

"Maybe I'll call Dad about this," I said.

"You can't," said Grandmere. "He's gone away with his new girlfriend. She's that...that interviewer—Beverly Bellerieve. Now, look Amelia, this will be your mother's wedding dress."

She held up a picture of a dress with a huge skirt. It was the kind of dress that my mom hates.

"Grandmere," I said. "You are working very hard. But my mom really doesn't want a big wedding."

Grandmere didn't listen to me. "Tell Amelia about the food for the wedding," she said to Vigo.

Vigo started describing the food. Then he described the music. After that, Grandmere and Vigo showed me the white and gold wedding invitations. I looked at the date on the invitations. It said: *Saturday, November 1st.*

"Wait a minute," I said. "Is the wedding *this* Saturday? That's in less than a week."

"Yes," said Grandmere.

"What if the guests are busy? What if they have other plans for that day?"

"The wedding has to be soon," said Vigo. "Your mother must be married quickly. In a few weeks, her pregnancy will show."

Grandmere has even told Vigo about my mom's baby! That's great. That's really great.

6

The Interview

Monday, October 27th. Evening

When I got home, I didn't tell my mom about Grandmere's plans for the wedding. My mom was in the bathroom. She was feeling sick because she was pregnant.

Mr Gianini was in the apartment. It was nearly time for my TV interview with Beverly Bellerieve. He switched on the TV, and we watched it together. The interview was horrible! It went like this:

A man's voice spoke at the beginning of the show. He was the announcer.

VOICE: It is Monday, the 27th of October. On *Twenty-Four/Seven* tonight is Beverly Bellerieve's interview with America's Princess. . .Mia Renaldo!

A picture of me and Beverly Bellerieve came on the TV. We were in the penthouse suite of the Plaza Hotel. Beverly looked at the TV camera and spoke.

BEVERLY: This is the amazing story of an ordinary teenage girl. She lives in New York City with her mom, Helen Thermopolis. Helen Thermopolis is an artist. A month ago, Mia was a normal teenager. Her life was filled with ordinary teenage things—things like homework and friends. Then one day, everything changed.

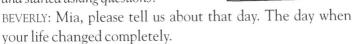

Then Beverly turned to me and started asking questions.

BEVERLY: Mia, please tell us about that day. The day when your life changed completely.

ME: We. . . I. . .was here at the Plaza with my dad. He told me two pieces of amazing news. First he said, "I am the Prince of Genovia." Then he said, "You are the Princess of Genovia and my heir. When I die, you'll become the ruler of Genovia."

BEVERLY: How did you feel about that news?

ME: I was really upset. Me! A princess! I didn't want anyone at school to know. I didn't want to be a freak like my friend Tina Hakim Baba. Tina's life is strange and lonely. Her father owns an oil company and he's very rich. Tina's parents worry about her safety. A bodyguard goes everywhere with her. He even comes to school. But that's what has happened to me too. I have a bodyguard. I'm a freak too, a huge freak.

BEVERLY: Oh, Mia, I can't believe that. Aren't you popular at school?

ME: No, I'm not. I'm not popular at all. Only the jocks—the boys who are very good at sport—are popular in my school. And the cheerleaders—the girls who shout and cheer while the jocks play—are popular too. But the popular people aren't my friends. I never get invited to their parties. Those are the really cool parties. Everyone drinks beer. And everyone makes out. . .er. . .kisses.

BEVERLY: Your grandmother—the Dowager Princess of Genovia—is helping you, isn't she? She's showing you how to be a princess.

ME: Oh, yes. She's giving me princess classes after school.

BEVERLY: Mia, you had some exciting news recently.

ME: Oh. Yes. I'm very excited. I've always wanted to be a big sister. But my mom and her boyfriend won't have a big wedding. . .

34

At that moment, my mom came out of the bathroom. She looked at the TV. She heard what I was saying on the film. Her mouth opened in shock. I had told the whole of America her private business!

We watched the rest of the TV show. As we watched, I became more and more embarrassed.

The interview ended like this:

BEVERLY: Amelia Mignonette Thermopolis Renaldo isn't a jock, or a cheerleader. But she is a very unusual girl. She's a modern princess. She is America's princess. Mia has the same problems as all American teenagers. But one day, she will rule a country. And next year, Mia will be a big sister. *Twenty-Four/Seven* is the show that heard Mia's exciting news first. Mia's mother, Helen Thermopolis, is expecting a baby in July. The father of Helen's baby is Frank Gianini— Mia's Algebra teacher at Albert Einstein High School. Frank and Helen will be having a small, quiet wedding.

———

Mom and Mr Gianini were nice to me. They weren't mad. But they were upset.

The phone rang. It was Lilly. My best friend *was* mad.

"You called us freaks," she said angrily. "What did you mean?"

"Lilly, I didn't call you a freak," I said.

"You said, 'Only jocks and cheerleaders are popular at my school.'" Lilly replied. "You said, 'I don't go around with the popular kids.' All your friends are unpopular. That's what you mean, isn't it? *Your* friends aren't cool. They're weird— they're freaks."

Then she hung up the phone.

A few seconds later, the phone rang again. It was my friend Shameeka.

"Mia," she said. "I invited you to my party. Do you remember?"

"Yes," I replied.

"Well, my dad won't let me have a party now," said Shameeka. "My dad said, 'Now parents of students at Albert Einstein know the truth. Mia Thermopolis has told us what happens at teenage parties in this area. Students have sex and drink beer at their parties. You can't have your party.'"

"Oh, Shameeka," I said. "I am *so* sorry."

Shameeka hung up the phone. The phone rang again. It was Tina Hakim Baba. Immediately, I apologized to her.

"I'm sorry, Tina," I said.

"Why are you sorry?" asked Tina happily. "You said my name on TV!"

"Er. . .I know." I had also called Tina a freak.

"I can't believe it!" she said. "It was so cool! It's the most exciting thing that has ever happened to me."

"You. . .you aren't mad at me?" I said. "Did your dad see the interview too?"

"Yes," said Tina. "He's very pleased. Now everyone knows about my bodyguard, Wahim. He protects me everywhere I go."

Tina hung up. The phone rang for the fourth time. It was Grandmere.

"Well," she said. "That was terrible, wasn't it?"

"I'm sorry, Grandmere," I said. "I didn't mean to say bad things about my school."

But Grandmere wasn't talking about my high school.

"That Bellerieve woman didn't show any pictures of

Genovia," she said. "We need more tourists to come to our country."

"Maybe I'll have to go to another school now," I said.

But Grandmere wasn't listening to me. Suddenly, she hung up the phone.

"Mia," my mom said. "The interview wasn't that bad. You told the truth about the jocks and the cheerleaders."

I went into my room and switched on my computer. I'd received a message from Michael Moscovitz. We had this chatroom conversation:

CracKing: Hi. I just saw you on TV. You were very good.

FtLouie: It was terrible.

CracKing: Well, you told the truth.

FtLouie: But Mom and Mr Gianini are upset. And Lilly and Shameeka are mad at me now.

CracKing: Don't worry about Lilly. She's jealous because more people watched your interview than her TV show. What are you doing on Saturday night?

I read the last line of his message again. Was Michael Moscovitz asking me out ON A DATE?

FtLouie: I don't know. Why?

CracKing: Well, Saturday is the day after Halloween. I'm going to a movie theater with some friends. We're going to see the ROCKY HORROR PICTURE SHOW. It's a really funny movie. Everyone is going to celebrate Halloween. We'll all wear scary costumes and crazy makeup. Do you want to come?

OK. Michael wasn't asking me out alone with him. But it will be nice to go out with him, and his friends. Then I remembered my mom's wedding.

FtLouie: Can I give you my answer later? Maybe I'm doing something with my family on Saturday night. I'll speak to you later.

CracKing: Sure. OK.

7

Surprise Visitors

Tuesday, October 27th. Algebra class

This morning, Principal Gupta—the head of Albert Einstein High School—asked me to come to her office.

"Are you very unhappy here at Albert Einstein?" she said. She looked worried. "Last night, in your TV interview, you said, 'I'm not popular.' But everyone in the school knows who you are."

"They know me because I'm a princess," I replied. "My story was printed in newspapers and magazines. Before that, very few people wanted to know me."

"You must join one of the school clubs," said Principal Gupta. "Then you'll meet more students. You'll have more friends."

"Principal Gupta," I said, "I don't have time for clubs. I don't have any time for myself after school finishes. Every afternoon, I have an extra Algebra class, and then I have a princess class with my grandmother. In the evenings, I do my homework."

Principal Gupta doesn't understand!

Late morning

Lilly's boyfriend, Boris Pelkowski, told me a secret about Lilly. She is secretly writing a book about our school.

I can't believe it. Why does Lilly only tell Boris her secrets? Why doesn't she tell me? Lilly and I have been best friends since elementary school. I tell Lilly everything. Well, almost everything. She didn't know about my mom and Mr Gianini's wedding, and their baby. She doesn't know about my feelings for her brother. And she doesn't know about my secret admirer. But I tell her nearly everything else.

Afternoon

Kenny, my partner in Biology class, spoke to me after class today.

"Are you doing anything on Saturday night?" he asked.

"I'm not sure," I replied. "Maybe I'll be eating dinner with my family."

"Well, I'm going to see a movie—the *Rocky Horror Picture Show*—with some friends from the Computer Club," he said. "Will you come too?"

"Is Michael Moscovitz one of your friends?" I asked.

"Yes," said Kenny.

6:00 p.m. In the limousine

I'm with Lars. We're going back to the apartment. I've just been to see Grandmere at the Plaza Hotel for my princess lesson. I walked into the suite and I had a shock. Lots of people were there. There were people talking about food and wine and flowers. Others were writing names on cards. Vigo was running about, telling everyone what to do. Grandmere was sitting and eating chocolates. Her little dog was sitting under her chair. He was shaking with fear.

"Ah, Amelia," said Grandmere. "Sit down. You can help me. Taste these chocolates. Which chocolates are best for the wedding guests?"

"Grandmere," I said, sitting down on a chair next to her. "Mom really won't be happy about these arrangements. She doesn't want a big wedding."

"Nonsense," said Grandmere loudly, in a scary voice. "This will be a wonderful event. I'm inviting lots of famous people. Many of them are very rich. Some of them are members of royal families."

It's impossible to argue with Grandmere. She never listens to me. So after my princess class, I went to my dad's hotel suite. I knocked on the door, but he didn't answer.

I went and talked to the hotel receptionist.

"The prince left the hotel a few hours ago," she said. "Beverly Bellerieve was with him."

10:00 p.m.

When I got home, there were strangers in the apartment. A family—a mom and a dad, and a boy with long blond hair— was in the dining room. They were sitting around the table. They had suitcases with them.

"Mia, don't you remember me?" asked the woman.

I stared at her. Suddenly I recognized the woman. My mouth fell open in shock. I couldn't believe it.

"*Grandmother Thermopolis?*" I said.

"Mia," said the woman. "You've never called me 'Grandmother.' I'm Mamaw."

My mom's mother, Mamaw, and my mom's father, Papaw, were in our apartment! I didn't recognize the young guy. He was dressed like a farmer. He was wearing a cotton shirt and denim overalls.

My mom's parents live in the state of Indiana. Indiana is hundreds of miles away from the state of New York. My grandparents live in a small town called Versailles. They've never been to New York City before.

My mom doesn't talk to her parents very often. We haven't visited Mamaw or Papaw for four years. When I was born, they were angry. This was because my mom didn't marry my father. My grandparents didn't help my mom when I was a baby. They didn't give her advice or any money.

I went to find my mom. She was in her bedroom. She was talking to my dad on the phone.

"Philippe," she was saying angrily, "your mother has invited my parents to New York. My *parents*, Philippe. *You know how I feel about my parents.*"

Then she saw me standing by the door.

"Are your grandparents still out there?" she whispered.

"Er. . .yes," I said. "Did you invite Mamaw and Papaw here?"

"No, I did *not!*" said my mom. "Grandmere Clarisse invited them. She's arranged a big wedding. It's going to be on SATURDAY!" Her voice was getting louder and louder. "Your Grandmere has invited hundreds of people—all her friends."

I felt terrible. I had forgotten to tell my mom about Grandmere's wedding plans.

41

Mom held out the phone toward me. "Your dad wants to talk to you," she said.

"Mia," said my dad. "I've arranged for your mother's parents to stay at the SoHo Grand Hotel. It's near your apartment. I'll send Lars with the limousine. Put the Thermopolises in the car. Lars will take them to the hotel."

"OK, Dad," I said. "But what about Grandmere's plans for the wedding?"

"Don't worry, Mia," he said. "I'll talk to Grandmere."

I returned to the living room. My grandparents were still sitting at the table. But the young guy was in the kitchen. He was looking inside the refrigerator.

"I'm hungry," he said. "Do you have anything to eat?"

"No," I said. "But you'll be able to order food from your hotel room."

"A *hotel room*?" said Mamaw. "Papaw, and your cousin Hank, and I, have come all the way from Indiana to see you. And you're going to put us in a *hotel*?"

I stared at the big blond guy. This was my cousin Hank? Hank is the son of my mom's sister, Marie. When I last saw Hank, he was about thirteen years old, and I was about ten. Hank had been a thin little boy. Now he was big, and more than six feet tall.

"That French woman—Clarisse Renaldo—called us," said Mamaw. "She told us to come here. She was going to pay for our visit. We can't pay for an expensive New York hotel."

"That's OK," I said. 'My father will pay your hotel bill."

"Oh, good," said Mamaw, smiling. "Let's go."

When Lars came with the limousine, I went with them to the hotel. But when we arrived at the SoHo Grand, I had another surprise.

42

"Mia, will you take Hank to school with you tomorrow?" asked Mamaw.

"Oh, you don't want to go to school with me, Hank," I said quickly. "You're on vacation."

"But I want to see what a New York City high school is like," said Hank.

When he said New York, Hank pronounced the words "Noo York." People from Indiana don't speak like people who live in New York. They have a different accent.

Then Hank whispered to me so that Mamaw didn't hear. "And I want to see what New York girls are like," he said.

So I had to say OK.

When I got home, Mom was lying on her bed. She was reading a magazine. Her eyes were red from crying.

"Oh, Mia," she said. "Come here and let me hug you. I'm sorry. I'm a terrible person. Grandmere Clarisse has made me angry and upset. She's planned everything. She's arranged *when* I will be married. She's chosen the *place* for my wedding. She's invited the *guests*. And Grandmere asked my parents to come to New York. They've come all the way from Indiana to see me. But I didn't want to speak to them. I didn't want them to stay here. I sent them to a hotel. But I didn't think about your feelings."

I felt sorry for my mom. Pregnancy should be a happy time. All this is Grandmere's fault. She's made my mom unhappy.

11:00 p.m.

Jo-C-rox has sent me another e-mail!

JoCrox: Dear Mia

I saw you on TV last night. You looked beautiful. Don't worry about your problems with some people at school.

You're really great! That's what most of us think.

Your Friend

I wrote back immediately.

FtLouie: Dear Friend,

Thank you very much. PLEASE tell me who you are. I won't tell anyone. I promise!

Mia

My secret admirer hasn't written back yet.

8

The Boy from Indiana

Wednesday, October 29th

Some surprising things happened when Hank came to school with me today. And these things made me look at my cousin more carefully. Suddenly, I realized something. Hank has changed a lot in four years.

Hank wears the kind of clothes that farmers wear—boots, a cotton shirt, and denim overalls. These are not the kind of clothes that young guys wear in New York. But Hank is big and strong and he has a really nice body. His hair is blond and his eyes are dark blue. In fact, Hank is gorgeous! All the girls stared at him as he walked through the school hall.

"Who is that sexy guy?" they asked me.

When Lana Weinberger first saw Hank, her eyes opened wide with surprise.

"Who's your friend?" she asked me.

"He's not my friend, he's my cousin," I replied.

"Well, you can be *my* friend," Lana said to Hank.

"Thanks," replied Hank. He looked down at Lana and smiled.

But the biggest surprise of all was Lilly. When she saw Hank, her mouth fell open and she couldn't speak. She just stared at him.

Afternoon

I don't believe what has happened today. *Lilly and Hank have disappeared.* Nobody knows where they are. Lilly's boyfriend, Boris, is really worried.

At lunch, Lilly asked Hank lots of questions about his life in Indiana.

"Do you have a girlfriend?" she asked.

"No, I don't," said Hank, "I was dating a girl called Amber. But we broke up two weeks ago."

Then Lilly started telling Hank about New York.

"You'll be bored here in school with Mia," she said. "Go visit some places in the city. There are lots of exciting things to see."

Since lunch, nobody has seen Lilly or Hank. Lilly will be in a lot of trouble. She's run away with Hank and she's missing her classes. Now I have to tell my grandparents. Their grandson has disappeared. What will Mamaw and Papaw say?

Algebra class

I told Lars, my bodyguard, what has happened.

"Lilly and Hank have disappeared. They've run away together," I said. "I'll call the police."

"No, wait," Lars said. Then he spoke to Mr Gianini. Mr Gianini agreed with Lars.

"Lilly is quite sensible," my Algebra teacher said. "She'll look after Hank."

But I'm really worried. Have Lilly and Hank fallen in

love with each other? Hank isn't very smart. But perhaps Lilly doesn't care about this. He *is* very good-looking.

7:00 p.m.

Hank and Lilly are OK. They're safe! Hank got back to the SoHo Grand hotel at about five o'clock. Lilly got back to her apartment at about the same time.

"We've been walking around the city," they said.

I don't believe them. But I have more important things to worry about. When I went to the Plaza Hotel for my princess class with Grandmere, my dad was outside her door. He was looking nervous.

"Mia," he said. "I have some bad news. Grandmere has already sent out the wedding invitations."

"*What?*" I said.

"Don't worry," said my dad. "I'll take care of everything."

My dad is a good man, but Grandmere is stronger than him. He won't be able to stop her.

I walked into Grandmere's suite. The royal wedding planner, Vigo, was with her.

"Lots of famous people have accepted our invitations," said Vigo proudly. "It'll be the biggest, most important wedding in New York this year."

I didn't say anything. I was thinking about Mom. She was going to be shocked when she saw hundreds of famous people at her wedding. None of them are *her* friends.

"Your dress for the wedding has arrived," said Vigo. And suddenly, he pulled a dress from a box. "What do you think?"

I've never seen such a beautiful dress. It was pink, with a huge skirt. As soon as I saw that dress, I wanted it. I wanted it more than anything in the world. And then I remembered. This dress was for my mom's wedding. The big

wedding that Grandmere had planned. I felt terrible. I'm a bad daughter. I can't wear the dress. My mom doesn't want a big wedding. I don't want this big wedding to happen. Only Grandmere wants this wedding.

"It *is* a beautiful dress," I thought. "I want Michael, or Jo-C-rox, to see me wearing it. I'll look like a real princess in this dress."

9

Secrets and Lies

Thursday, October 30th. English class

Hank didn't come to school with me today. He called the apartment early in the morning.

"I'm sick," he said.

Last night, Mr Gianini took Mom, me, Mamaw, Papaw and Hank to dinner at a famous restaurant. Everybody had a very good time and they ate a lot. If Hank is sick, I'm not surprised.

When Hank didn't come to school today, all the girls were very disappointed. Only Boris was happy. He's very jealous of Hank. Does Lilly like Hank more than Boris? I don't know.

Afternoon

Lilly and Hank have disappeared AGAIN! Before lunch, my mom called Lars on his cellphone. Mamaw had spoken to Mom because Hank was missing from his hotel room. Mamaw was worried about her grandson.

"Lars, did Hank go to school with Mia today?" asked my mom.

"No," said Lars.

Then, at lunchtime, Lilly said, "I'm feeling sick. I'm going home."

I don't believe what Lilly said. She isn't sick. She's gone to meet Hank somewhere. That's what I think. What *are* Hank and Lilly doing? Do they love each other? Are they having sex?

7:00 p.m. In the limousine

I've just had another shock. Now I'm in the limousine with Lars. He's driving me to my apartment.

When I went to Grandmere's suite today, Mamaw was there. Mamaw and Grandmere were sitting on couches and drinking tea. They were talking about someone.

Vigo was speaking on the phone. He was making more arrangements for the wedding.

"She was always very stubborn," Mamaw was saying. "She never takes advice or listens to anyone."

"I am *not* stubborn!" I said.

"Don't enter the room in that rude way, Amelia," said Grandmere. She spoke in French. "Come here and say hello to me properly."

I went and kissed Grandmere on both of her cheeks. Then I kissed Mamaw on both of her cheeks too. Mamaw laughed and said, "We don't say hello like that in Indiana."

"Now, Shirley," Grandmere said to Mamaw in English.

48

"What were we talking about?"

"Helen is being difficult about this wedding and I'm not surprised," said Mamaw. "But Papaw and I are very happy. Frank Gianini is very nice."

So they weren't talking about me. They were talking about my mom! They're arranging this wedding together!

"Shirley, we both agree," said Grandmere. "This wedding will take place. It must take place."

"Oh, certainly, Your Highness," said Mamaw.

"But Grandmere," I said. "Mom doesn't want—"

"Vigo!" shouted Grandmere. "Bring those shoes for the princess! She'll wear them with her new pink dress on Saturday."

Vigo came toward me with a pair of pink shoes. They were the same color as my dress. They were the prettiest shoes that I've ever seen.

"Aren't they lovely?" said Vigo. "Put them on."

The beautiful shoes fit me perfectly.

"It's sad," said Grandmere. "Your mother doesn't want this wedding. We'll have to send the shoes back to the store."

"Can I keep them for another time?" I asked.

"Oh, no," said Grandmere quickly. "You can only wear pink shoes at a wedding."

I'm worried. My dad promised to stop this wedding. But he hasn't done anything. He won't be able to stop Grandmere. She has arranged for a limousine to come to our apartment on Saturday. The driver will pick up me, Mom and Mr Gianini. Will my mom refuse to get into the car on November 1st?

9:00 p.m.

Mr Gianini has moved into our apartment. He brought with him a table with a football game on it, and a TV. The football table is great. I've already played nine games.

"You can call me 'Frank' now, Mia," he said.

But it's very difficult for me to call Mr Gianini "Frank." He's my Algebra teacher.

I asked my mom about the wedding on Saturday. But she just smiled.

"Don't worry about that, Mia," she said.

Mom didn't say anything more. She didn't want to talk about the wedding. So I called Lilly. Her phone line was busy, so I sent her an instant message on the Internet.

When Lilly and I chat online, Lilly uses the name "WmnRule." It means "women are cool."

FtLouie: Where did you and Hank go to today?

WmnRule: I'm not going to tell you. It's a secret.

FtLouie: Lilly, I'm worried about you. You missed classes today. And Boris was upset too.

WmnRule: Well, Boris has to trust me. And you must trust me too, Mia.

Suddenly I received a new message—from Jo-C-rox!

JoCrox: Are you coming to see the ROCKY HORROR SHOW movie?

Jo-C-rox is going to the *Rocky Horror* movie on Saturday. Michael is going to the *Rocky Horror* movie too. Michael MUST BE Jo-C-rox.

I felt really happy and excited. I wanted to run around the room. I wanted to scream and laugh at the same time. I wrote back immediately.

FtLouie: Yes, I want to come to the movie.

10

Hank's Dream Comes True

Friday, October 31st. Halloween

I was completely wrong about Lilly Moscovitz. At lunch, I found out the truth about her and Hank.

We were all sitting in the school cafeteria—me and my bodyguard Lars, Tina Hakim Baba, and her bodyguard Wahim, Lilly, Boris, and our friends, Shameeka and Ling Su.

Suddenly, someone walked up to our table. We looked up. A tall, very handsome young man was standing there. We all stared in surprise. It was Hank! But he looked *very* different. Everyone in the cafeteria stopped talking. They were all looking at him.

Hank was wearing a black sweater, a long black leather coat, black jeans, and black boots. His blond hair had been cut short. He looked like the actor, Keanu Reeves, in the film, *The Matrix*.

"Hello, Mia," said my cousin, sitting down beside me.

Hank's clothes were different, but his voice was different too. It was deeper. He didn't pronounce words like a person from Indiana. He no longer had an Indiana accent.

"So," Lilly said to him. "What happened?"

"Well," Hank said in his new, deep voice. "I have to thank you, Lilly. I got the job. I'm going to be a model. A famous fashion company wants me to model underwear. Pictures of me will soon be in magazines and on TV." He smiled a huge smile.

"Mia," he said, turning to me, "Your friend has done something that no one has ever done for me in my life."

What *had* Lilly done?

"When I was a young boy, I had a dream about being a model," said Hank. "I wanted to be a fashion model. But everyone laughed at me. When I told Lilly about my dream, she helped me. Now my dream has come true. I'm going to be a model. I'm going to be rich and famous."

"I only helped you a little, Hank," said Lilly. "I told you where to go. And I told you who to meet. You did the rest yourself."

Suddenly Hank stood up and pulled Lilly to her feet. Then he kissed her for a long time. Everyone stared at them.

When Hank let Lilly go, she sat down slowly.

"I'm never going back to Versailles with Mamaw and Papaw," Hank said to me. "Please tell them that."

Then he turned, and he started to walk out of the cafeteria. But just as Hank reached the door, Boris stood up. He grabbed Hank's arm.

"Hey, you!" Boris said. "Lilly is *my* girl, not yours."

Two boys were arguing because of Lilly! It was very romantic. I want a boy to call me *his* girl. I want *Michael* to call me his girl.

Then Boris hit Hank in the face. But Boris hurt his own hand. He didn't hurt Hank.

Afternoon

I used Lars's cellphone to call Mamaw and Papaw at their hotel. Mamaw answered the call.

"It's me," I said. "I'm calling with news about Hank."

"WHERE IS HE?" shouted Mamaw.

"Mamaw," I said. "Hank is OK. He's going to be a model. He's got a contract with one of the best modeling agencies in New York. He's going to model underwear. He's going to be very famous."

"UNDERWEAR!" Mamaw shouted. "My grandson is going to model *underwear*! Mia, tell Hank to call me RIGHT NOW. He's in BIG TROUBLE."

"OK, Mamaw," I said. "Er. . .is the wedding still going to take place tomorrow? Did you talk to my mom?"

"Of course," said Mamaw. "Everything is ready."

"Really?" I said. I was very surprised. "Has Mom agreed to the plans? Will she be at the Gold and White Room at the Plaza on Saturday?"

"Yes, she'll be there," said Mamaw.

I hung up the phone. I felt sad and a little disappointed. I was sad for Mom, because she didn't want a big wedding. And I was sad for myself, because I didn't want to go to the wedding on Saturday. I wanted to go to the *Rocky Horror* movie with Michael.

Later, I talked with Lilly about Hank. Michael was there too.

ME: Why did you help Hank become a model, Lilly?

LILLY: Hank had a dream about becoming a model. So I helped him. I gave him some advice about fashion. I helped him to speak without his Indiana accent. Then he went to the modeling agency. They said, "You're tall and you have an excellent body. Your face, skin, eyes, teeth and hair are very good." Then a photographer took some photos of Hank. The pictures were great! The agency became very excited. The next day, they gave him a job.

ME: Why was Hank's visit to the agency a big secret? Why didn't you tell me about it?

LILLY: Because he didn't want you to laugh at him. Hank is your cousin. You don't see him as other people see him. But he's a very special person. He'll do great things. His dream can come true.

MICHAEL: Yeah. He'll model underwear.

LILLY: You're jealous, Michael. Hank is going to be a supermodel!

—

Michael didn't say anything else to me all day. Is he Jo-C-rox, my secret admirer? Why won't he tell me?

<u>Five reasons why Michael won't tell me</u>

1. He's shy. He can't tell me his real feelings.

2. He thinks that I don't like him.

3. He's thought about me, and now he doesn't like me.

4. He doesn't want a freshman to be his girlfriend. He's older than me. He's a senior.

5. He isn't Jo-C-rox.

54

11

My Mom's Wedding Day

Saturday, November 1st, 7:00 p.m. The Plaza Hotel

It's been a *very* strange day. When I woke up this morning, the apartment was very quiet. I went to my mom's bedroom and knocked on the door. But nobody answered. So I opened the door and went inside. No one was there!

A few minutes later, the phone rang. It was my dad.

"Dad, Mom has disappeared," I said. "And Mr Gianini isn't here either. Where are they?"

"Don't worry, Mia," said my dad. "Your mother is OK. She's written you a letter. I have it here. You can have it at eight o'clock tonight."

"But Dad, the wedding is at eight o'clock tonight."

"I know," said my dad. "I have to go now, Mia."

"No, Dad, wait—"

But my dad hung up the phone. Then it rang again. It was Grandmere.

"Are you and your mother ready?" she asked. "We're all going to the beauty salon. You have to get your hair and makeup done."

"Er. . .Mom's left already," I said.

"Well," said Grandmere. "The limousine is coming to your apartment at ten o'clock to pick you up."

When the limousine arrived, Grandmere was sitting in it with Mamaw. "Your mother has gone to another beauty salon," said Grandmere. "Your father told me."

We went to Grandmere's favorite beauty salon—Chez Paolo. We stayed there all day. When we left, our hair and makeup looked beautiful. Then we went back to the Plaza

Hotel and I put on my lovely pink dress and shoes.

I'm sitting here in a little room, waiting for my mom.

9:00 p.m.

MY MOM AND MR GIANINI ARE MARRIED!

At 7:45 the wedding guests began to arrive at the White and Gold Room. Hundreds of famous people came. There were rock stars, millionaires, and film actors. There were members of royal families and beautiful models.

At eight o'clock, I asked my dad for my mom's letter. I read it and then I had to sit down. I couldn't believe what I read. Then my dad went to the front of the room and made a speech to the guests.

"Thank you all for coming here tonight," he said. "Unfortunately, the wedding will not take place this evening.

This morning, Helen Thermopolis and Frank Gianini eloped. They flew to Mexico and got married secretly."

Grandmere screamed and almost fell from her chair. Vigo ran to help her.

"But please stay and have dinner with us," continued my dad. "There is lots of wonderful food and wine in the ballroom. And thank you again for coming."

The guests were very surprised. They stood up and went into the ballroom. I read the letter from my mom again.

My Dear Mia,

You will be reading this letter at 8 o'clock. By that time, Frank and I will be married. I couldn't tell you our plans before. I didn't want your grandmother to ask you questions about us.

You're a wonderful daughter, and you've helped me a lot during this crazy time. This new baby will be very lucky. He or she will have a wonderful big sister.

Your loving Mom

I wasn't shocked by the news of Mom's secret marriage. It's very romantic. I was shocked because my father helped my mom and Mr Gianini. And my dad stopped Grandmere's plans. My dad has always been frightened of Grandmere.

I went up to my father and put my arms around him. I hugged him tightly.

"You did it, Dad!" I said, laughing. "Grandmere will be really mad when she knows the truth."

"Why are you surprised, Mia?" he said. "I'm not frightened of my mother. She isn't as bad as you think."

Just then, Vigo came over to us.

"Your Highness," he said to my dad, "your mother—the Dowager Princess Clarisse—is in her hotel suite. She won't come out. She's upset and embarrassed."

My dad and I went up to Grandmere's penthouse suite. My dad knocked on the door.

"Mother," he called. "It's Philippe. Please open this door at once."

There was no reply.

"Dad," I said quietly. "Let me speak to her."

"Grandmere, it's me, Mia," I called through the door. "Mom and Mr Gianini eloped and I'm really sorry. But Mom didn't want this big wedding. I told you that."

There was still no reply.

"Grandmere," I said. "You're not behaving like a princess. A princess must always be brave, even if things go wrong. You taught me that. A princess must never hide her face. Come down to the ballroom. Come to the party and speak to your guests."

Suddenly the door opened and Grandmere came out. She was wearing a purple dress, and she had jewels in her hair.

"Of course I'm going back to the party," she said. "I had to put on more makeup. That's why I came up here."

I looked at my dad and my dad looked at me.

"Of course, Grandmere," I said.

Then Grandmere did a surprising thing. She held my arm. Then I held my dad's arm. The three of us stood in the hallway, joined together. It was a very special moment.

Sunday, November 2nd, 2:00 p.m.

Everybody had a very good time at the party. Later in the

evening, Hank arrived. Mamaw and Papaw were pleased to see him, and so were all the girls. He looked gorgeous! He even asked Grandmere to dance.

At ten o'clock, Lars's cellphone rang. It was my mom calling from Mexico. She and Mr Gianini were drinking champagne on a beach. She was really happy. I talked to her quietly because I didn't want Grandmere to hear.

A few minutes later, my dad came up to me. "Mia, don't you want to meet your friends tonight?" he asked.

I hadn't forgotten about the *Rocky Horror* movie. But I remembered Grandmere's words to me in princess classes. "Your family is more important than your friends," she had said.

But now Grandmere was happy. She had forgotten about me. She was dancing with a famous film actor.

"Yes," I said to my dad. "I do want to meet my friends."

"Well, you can go," he said.

Lars drove me to the *Rocky Horror* movie theater. When we got there, we drove up and down the street, looking for my friends.

Suddenly I saw Lilly. Boris and Michael were with her. Kenny Showalter and Michael's other friends from the Computer Club were there too. They were all dressed in weird costumes. They looked like characters from horror films and ghost stories. I got out of the car and ran toward them. Michael stared at me.

"I don't have a horror costume," I said, looking down at my dress. "I'm sorry."

"You look really. . .You look really. . ." he said.

Then he stopped. What was he going to say? Didn't I look OK? Did my dress look stupid?

We sat and watched the movie. I was sitting in a seat between Michael and Kenny. Lars sat behind me. Michael didn't say much. Kenny tried to talk to me, but I was only thinking about Michael. I sat beside him in the dark, and it was wonderful.

The movie lasted for two hours and it was really good. Afterwards, we went to a café called, Round the Clock. I sat between Michael and Kenny. Everyone talked very loudly.

Suddenly, Kenny whispered something in my ear.

"Have you had any interesting mail lately?" he asked.

Then I realized the truth. Michael wasn't Jo-C-rox. Kenny was my secret admirer! Kenny is a really nice boy and I like him. But he isn't as sexy and attractive as Michael Moscovitz.

I looked at Kenny and I tried to smile. "Oh, Kenny," I said. "Are you Jo-C-rox?"

"Yes," said Kenny. "Will you come on a date with me, Mia?"

I was very disappointed. Kenny is a good friend. But do I want him to be my boyfriend? No. I'm in love with Michael. But I didn't want to hurt Kenny's feelings. I spoke kindly and quietly to him.

"OK, Kenny," I said. "I'll go out with you."

Kenny smiled and put his arm around my shoulders. Michael saw Kenny putting his arm around me and smiling.

Suddenly Michael stood up. There was a weird expression on his face. "I'm tired," he said. "Let's go home."

"What's wrong, Michael?" said Lilly in a surprised voice.

"I'm tired, too," I said. "Lars, please can we go to the car?"

"Mia, can I call you later?" asked Kenny.

Lilly looked at me. Then she looked at Kenny. Then she looked at Michael. Suddenly she stood up too.

"Come on," she said to Boris. "It's time to go."

Lilly, Boris, Michael and I went in the limousine with Lars. Michael sat beside me in the car. He was silent and I felt terrible. Everything had gone wrong.

At last, we arrived at the Moscovitzes' apartment.

Suddenly, Michael turned toward me. "You look really nice in that dress," he said.

I smiled at him. Suddenly I felt happy again.

———

Now I'm sitting in Grandmere's suite at the Plaza Hotel. Maybe things aren't so bad. Soon, I'm going to have a new baby brother or sister. And I've got a really nice new stepfather—Mr Gianini.

Kenny called at midday. I'm going to see a Japanese movie with him at four o'clock. After that, I'm going to Lilly's place. I'm going to spend the night there. We're going to watch a video of my favorite movie—*Dirty Dancing*.

Yesterday was a special experience. Maybe I'll see Michael at breakfast tomorrow morning. That will be better than anything.

Points for Understanding

1

Who are these people?
  (a) Fat Louie
  (b) Michael Moscovitz
  (c) Philippe Renaldo
  (d) Frank Gianini
  (e) Grandmere
  (f) Kenny Showalter

2

Why are these numbers important?
  (a) 98.4°F
  (b) Twenty-Four/Seven

3

What are the e-mail names of these people?
  (a) Mia
  (b) Michael
  (c) Mia's secret admirer

4

Mia makes a bad mistake and she does something stupid.
  (a) What are these things?
  (b) Where do they happen?

5

Grandmere is arranging Helen Thermopolis's wedding.
  (a) Who is helping Grandmere?
  (b) Which things has Grandmere planned?
  (c) What does Mia think about this?

6

Give the meanings of these words:
    (a) jocks
    (b) cheerleaders
    (c) freaks
    (d) making out
Why they are important in this chapter?

7

1 Who hasn't Mia seen for four years? Why?
2 Who is upset and angry?

8

Mia loses something and she is given something. What are they?

9

This chapter is called "Secrets and Lies." Why?

10

Who comes into the cafeteria? Why does everyone stare at him?

11

Lots of things happen on the day after Halloween.
    (a) Who is happy?
    (b) Who is disappointed?
    (c) Who is upset and embarrassed?
    (d) Who is quiet?
    (e) Who is surprised?

Exercises

Multiple Choice 1

Tick the correct answers to these questions about Princess Amelia Mignonette Grimaldi Thermopolis Renaldo.

Q1 What do most people usually call her?
   a Mia ✓   b Mignonette   c Amelia

Q2 How old is she in this book?
   a 14   b 15   c 16

Q3 Where does she go to school?
   a Genovia   b New York   c Idaho

Q4 How tall is she?
   a 180cm   b 6 feet   c 5 feet 9 inches

Q5 What is her mother's job?
   a Artist   b Teacher   c Model

Q6 What is her father's title?
   a Mister   b Doctor   c Prince

Q7 What is the name of her cat?
   a Rommel   b Fat Louie   c Vigo

Q8 Who is her best friend?
   a Lilly   b Beverly   c Lana

Q9 Who is the Dowager Princess Clarisse?
   a Her aunt   b Her mother   c Her grandmother

Q10 Amelia is a member of which royal family?
   a Andorran   b Monegasque   c Genovian

Story Outline

Complete the gaps. Use each word (or phrase) in the box once.

ADDRESS   Prince   Earth   PETS   full   salon   AGE
artist   City   DESCRIPTION   name   pounds   BOYFRIEND
cat   Genovia   NAME   call   sometimes   light   PARENTS
curly   everyone   show   BEST FRIEND   meat   large   tall
SCHOOL GRADE   gray   blond

[1] ...NAME...: My full name is Princess Amelia Mignonette Grimaldi
Thermopolis Renaldo of [2] ...Genovia........... . When people speak
to me they [3] .... me, "Your Highness." In America,
I'm [4] .... called "Princess Mia." A month ago,
[5] .... called me Mia (or Amelia) Thermopolis. My
friends call me "Mia."

[6] ....: 14

[7] ....: Freshman – ninth grade.

[8] ....: I'm five feet and nine inches

[9] .... My eyes are [10] .... and my

feet are too [11] .... My hair is short and very

[12] .... The real color of my hair is

[13] .... brown. But last month I went to a beauty

[14] .... Paolo, the stylist, cut my hair and colored it

[15] .... Also, I'm a vegetarian – I don't eat

[16] ....

[17] ....: My mother's [18] .... is

Helen Thermopolis. She's an [19] .... My father's

[20] .... name is Artur Christoff Philippe Gerard

Grimaldi Renaldo. He is the [21] .... of

Genovia.

[22] ....: Fat Louie – an orange and white [23] .... Fat

Louie is eight years old and he weighs 25 [24] ....

[25] ....: Lilly Moscovitz. Lilly is very smart and

she's interested in politics and ecology. She cares about people and what

happens to the planet [26] .... She makes films

about the people of New York, and their problems. She has her own TV

[27] .... – 'Lilly Tells It Like It Is.'

[28] ....: I don't have one.

[29] ....: 1005 Thompson Street, Apartment 4A, New

York. I've lived all my life in New York [30] .... with

my mother.

What Happened Next?

Number the sentences in the correct order.

[1] Mia is ill and can't go to school.

☐ When she is starting to feel better she gets a love letter from a secret admirer.

☐ Lilly gives Mia some homework and they watch a movie together.

☐ The doctor gives her a prescription for some medicine.

☐ Because she is ill her mom stays at home and looks after her.

☐ After Mia gets her love letter she is visited by Lilly.

☐ After she has taken her medicine she starts to feel better.

☐ Her mom thinks Mia is getting worse so she takes her to see the doctor.

☐ After watching the movie with Lilly, Mia reads her e-mails.

☐ Mia takes her medicine, but hopes she stays ill, as she doesn't want to do an interview.

Word Focus

Complete the gaps with *or, but* or *and*.

1   Helen is pregnant .. *and* .. Mia is going to be a big sister.

2   Helen asked who her secret admirer was .... they wouldn't tell her.

3   Mia turned on her computer .... read her e-mails.

4   Mia thought JoCrox was either Michael .... Lilly.

5   Tina .... Ling Su are both Mia's friends.

6   Mia liked the dress .... the shoes she was shown for the wedding.

7   Helen and Frank could get married at the Plaza .... elope to Mexico.

8   Hank wanted to stay in New York .... Mamaw wanted him to come home.

9   Mia had to hurry .... she would miss the movie.

10 Kenny is nice .... Mia loves Michael.

Words From the Story

Unjumble the letters to find words from the story. The meanings are given to help you.

Example	nregpnat
MEANING	going to have a baby
ANSWER	*pregnant*

1
MEANING
ANSWER

rnilPipac
the head of an American High School
....

2
MEANING
ANSWER

agoDrwe rsinPsce
a princess whose husband is dead
....

3
MEANING
ANSWER

ngsile npetar
a person who raises a child on their own
....

4
MEANING

ANSWER

mafenshr
a junior student at a high school or college (male or female)
....

5
MEANING
ANSWER

acernc
a serious illness
....

6
MEANING

ANSWER

ievitwner
a meeting at which a person talks about himself or herself
....

7
MEANING
ANSWER

nedggae
going to be married
....

8	njku odof
MEANING	unhealthy food such as soft drinks and burgers and chips
ANSWER	....

9	eopel
MEANING	to run away together and get married
ANSWER	....

Making Sentences 1

Match the two parts of each sentence.

My friends are also	to send messages to each other.
Her face was pale and	and rushed over to me.
Michael and I often use computers	in the ninth grade.
My interview is going to	with him, and his friends.
Vigo jumped up from his chair	Grandmere is stronger than him.
But it will be nice to go out	her hair looked terrible.
My mum doesn't talk	and it was really good.
My dad is a good man, but	be shown on Monday night.
I wasn't shocked by the news of	to her parents very often.
The movie lasted for two hours	Mom's secret marriage.

True or False?

Write T (True) or F (False).

1 Mia thinks that Michael isn't interested in her. $\boxed{T}$
2 Frank tells Mia that her mother is pregnant.   ☐
3 Tina Hakim Baba sends messages to Mia as JoCrox.   ☐
4 Lilly was making a film about teenagers behaving badly.   ☐
5 Helen and Frank want a big wedding.   ☐
6 Mia is embarrassed about her interview with Beverly Bellerieve.   ☐
7 Nobody has fun at the wedding party.   ☐
8 Mamaw Thermopolis and Clarisse Renaldo are sisters.   ☐
9 Hank wanted to be a writer.   ☐
10 Mia agrees to go out with Kenny.   ☐

Making Sentences 2

Write questions for the answers.

Example	**Where** *does Grandmere Clarise stay in New York?*
ANSWER	Grandmere Clarise stays at the Plaza Hotel in New York.

Q1 *What*
A1 Grandmere wants to arrange a big wedding for Frank and Helen.

Q2 *Who*
A2 Grandmere has invited many rich and famous people to the wedding.

Q3 *Who*
A3 Philippe Renaldo will pay for the wedding.

Q4 *Where*
A4 Helen's parents live in Versailles, Idaho.

Q5 *What*
A5 Cousin Hank hopes to become a male model.

Q6 *How*
A6 Grandmere found out about Frank and Helen when Amelia told Beverly Bellerieve.

Q7 *What*
A7 Philippe asked Mia if Frank was living with Helen.

Q8 *What*
A8 Frank told Mia to call him Frank.

Q9 *Why*
A9 Mia has a problem because Mr Frank Gianini is her teacher.

Q10 *Where*
A10 Frank and Helen get married in Mexico.

Chose the Word

Circle the correct words.

Mamaw

My mom's parents [1] **leave / live** in Idaho. They [2] **are / have been** farmers all their [3] **lives / leaves**. The name of the town [4] **where / which** they live is Versailles. It's a very small [5] **place / plaice**. It's [6] **a long / along** way from Versailles to New York. This is the [7] **first / once** time that my grandparents have [8] **arrived / come** to New York.

Papaw

Mom's parents [9] **were / was** angry when I was [10] **born / baby**. My mother [11] **was not / did not** married. My grandparents [12] **would / should** not help my mother. In fact, they [13] **would / could** not [14] **speak / spoke** to her for ten years. Mom [15] **tried / tryed** to call them but they put the phone [16] **down / up**. Now, mom [17] **has not / does not** [18] **want / wanted** them at her wedding. Grandmere Clarisse has [19] **invited / invitationed** them to the Plaza Hotel. Frank Gianini's parents [20] **are / were** dead and he has no brothers and sisters.

Grandmere

Grandmere Clarisse [21] **has come / comes** from an old and rich family. She was [22] **engaged / wedded** to the Prince of Genovia when she was 20 years old. She [23] **had never / never** met him before. Her father [24] **told / said** her the name of her husband. There was no [25] **discussion / discussions**. 'He is a prince,' her father [26] **told / said**. 'You [27] **are / will be** a princess when you are [28] **marry / married**.' That was that. The wedding [29] **took / had taken** place two years later. Since then, Grandmere [30] **lived / has lived** happily ever after. She had [31] **one / single** child – Philippe. Her husband [32] **died / dead** in 1989 and her son Philippe became Prince of Genovia.

Multiple Choice 2

Tick the true statement.

Q1 a Mia lives at 1005 Jackson Street, Apartment 4A, New York
b Mia lives at 1278 Jackson Street, Apartment 4A, New York
c Mia lives at 1005 Thompson Street, Apartment 4A, New York ✓

Q2 a Mia's interview is filmed at the Plaza Hotel.
b Mia's interview is filmed at Albert Einstein High School.
c Mia's interview is filmed at Helen's apartment.

Q3 a Grandmere thinks the interview will teach Mia to be obedient.
b Grandmere thinks the interview will make Mia a celebrity.
c Grandmere thinks the interview will be good for tourism in
Genovia.

Q4 a Lilly asks Mia to throw an eggplant out of a window.
b Lilly forces Mia to drop an eggplant out of a window.
c Lilly dares Mia to drop an eggplant out of a window.

Q5 a Mia calls all her friends "unpopular".
b Mia calls all her friends "cheerleaders".
c Mia calls all her friends "jocks".

Q6 a Principal Gupta thinks Mia should stay away from school.
b Principal Gupta thinks Mia should join one of the school clubs.
c Principal Gupta thinks Mia should dress more formally.

Q7 a Lilly and Hank disappear together during school.
b Lilly and Hank disappear together during Mia's interview.
c Lilly and Hank disappear together during Helen and Frank's
wedding.

Q8 a Hank punches Boris.
b Boris punches Hank.
c Hank and Boris punch Michael.

Q9 a No one dresses up for *The Rocky Horror Picture Show*.
b Everyone dresses up for *The Rocky Horror Picture Show*.
c Everyone except Mia dresses up for *The Rocky Horror Picture Show*.

Published by Macmillan Heinemann ELT
Between Towns Road, Oxford OX4 3PP
Macmillan Heinemann ELT is an imprint of
Macmillan Publishers Limited
Companies and representatives throughout the world
Heinemann is a registered trademark of Pearson Education, used under licence.

ISBN 978 0 2300 3748 9
ISBN 978 1 4050 8066 8 (with CD pack)

The Princess Diaries: Take Two by Meg Cabot. Copyright © Meg Cabot 2001

First published 2000 by HarperCollins Children's Books, USA a division of
HarperCollinsPublishers. First published in UK by Macmillan Children's
Books, a division of Macmillan Publishers Limited

Meggin Cabot asserts her right to be identified as the author of the
original work of which this Graded Reader is an adaptation

This retold version by Anne Collins for Macmillan Readers
Text Copyright © Macmillan Publishers Limited 2005
Design and illustration © Macmillan Publishers Limited 2005

This version first published 2005

Illustrated by Karen Donnelly
Cover illustration by Nicola Slater
Original cover template design by Jackie Hill
Additional design by Anne Sherlock

Printed in Thailand
2014 2013 2012
8 7 6 5

with CD pack
2014 2013 2012
11 10 9 8